NORTH ANTRIM

Volume Two

A COLLECTION OF PHOTOGRAPHS

By

Arthur   Ward

This publication was kindly sponsored by

RADISSON ROE PARK
HOTEL AND GOLF RESORT

ROSSWILSONARTIST.COM

Published by Arthur Ward

Photographs copyright
Arthur Ward 1998

Design & Layout
Arthur Ward

British Cataloguing in publication Data:

Ward, Arthur - North Antrim, Vol.2.

ISBN: 0-9533577-1-6

Printing, binding and colour reproduction
by J.C. Print Ltd. Belfast

The author wishes to thank the sponsors of
this publication.

Website: www.northantrim.com

Cover Photo: Knockans - Cushendall

Swans on the River Margie

INTRODUCTION

Welcome to volume two which I hope will inspire you as much as the subject matter has inspired me. This volume completes my original idea to photograph the North Antrim coast and inland areas from Portrush to Glenariffe. Together the two books are as much a personal tribute to the places that I have explored, enjoyed and drawn inspiration from throughout my life, as they are a photographic journey and record of the landscape known as North Antrim.

 There have been many changes to the landscape of the area since volume one, many locations now bear the scars of large developments, single storey rural cottages have been transformed into two and three storey townhouses and apartment blocks now rise in disharmony with their natural environment. Ironically, the cost of this surge in commercial exploitation is the erosion of the very essence that attracts and inspires people to visit the area in the first instance.

Any visitor who has passed through the area, any stranger who has come to settle here or like myself, any indigenous native will readily know what an unique and beautiful landscape we have been privileged with to enjoy and live within.

Those of you who have ventured off the main roads to explore will have already discovered the endless treasures and lasting memories of this landscape. It is quite amazing that no matter how many times we may visit a location, or how familiar we become with it, we will always be surprised by a new vista or experience, an intriguing fact that inspires and teaches the eye to see, the heart to feel and the imagination to wander.

The images in this book will take you from Ballycastle to Rathlin Island, from Fair Head to Glenariffe and cover the hills, mountains and glens that lie between. I have purposely skimmed over the towns and villages in both volumes to concentrate on the landscape and subject matter within them that conveys the essence of the locations to me. For those of you who are technically minded the photographs were taken with a standard Nikon 35mm camera, a 28/70mm and 70/300mm as used in volume one. Film stock was Fuji Velvia and Astia colour reversal. A few images were also taken with a Canon G3 digital, a new avenue of exploration for me.

Arthur Ward

Over Glenshesk to Rathlin Island

Ballycastle Seafront and Knocklayde Mountain

Ballycastle Marina

Ballycastle lies at the outflow of the glens of Taisie and Shesk overlooked by the mountain of Knocklayde. Sorley Boy MacDonnell was born here in 1505 at Dunanenie Castle and died there in 1585, he is interred in the vaults of Bonamargie Friary built by the McQuillens in the late 1400s, originally thatched this exceptional ruin consists of a chapel, gatehouse, cloisters, living quarters, vaults and a graveyard. After the friars left in the late 16th century, a Julia McQuillen is said to have taken up residency. She prophesised many events and became known as the Black Nun, a small holed cross near the west gable of the chapel is said to mark her grave.

The river Shesk and Carey combine to form the Margie river, legend tells of how the Children of Lir sheltered here from winter storms. Turned into swans by their stepmother they were exiled to spend 900 years in three parts of Ireland, one being the Cold Seas of Moyle, their release and transformation back to human form is said to have heralded the arrival of Christianity to Ireland.

Rising over six hundred feet, the impressive face of Fair Head dominates the view from the seafront where a modern marina provides safe anchorage and a ferry service to Rathin Island and Scotland. Eight miles long and four miles out, Rathlin lies like a stepping stone between north Antrim and the Scottish Islands, with three lighthouses the Island is renowned for its natural environment.

Early Sunrise - Bonamargie Friary

Fair Head from Ballycastle Beach

Basking Seals and Ferry - Rathlin Island

Inner harbour and old ferry - circa 1995

Inner Quay and Manor House - Rathlin Island

Rathlin is steeped in history which is evident in the standing stones, cairns, cashels, passage tombs and ancient ruins that are scattered over its landscape. One famous visitor was the Scottish king Robert the Bruce who in 1307 while taking refuge from the English in a cave, was inspired by the efforts of a spider trying to reach the roof. He later returned to Scotland to rebuild his army which finally defeated the army of Edward II at the Battle of Bannockburn in 1314.

The natural environment of the island is unique; you'll find seals basking on rocks at Rue Point, Puffins nesting at Bull Point and buzzards soaring above rare orchids over Altacarry Head. The island retains a quiet, unique character removed from the rush and bustle of modern day life, here you can easily slip into a timeless ambience.

Rathlin has seen scores of vessels wrecked around its shores, one of these was H.M.S. Drake which lies in Church Bay. This 14,000 ton armoured cruiser sank on October 1st 1917 and was one of three ships torpedoed within hours of each other by the German submarine U79. The other two were the destroyer H.M.S. Brisk and the S.S. Lugano, en route from Norfolk, Virginia to Liverpool, with cotton and steel.

Three miles from Rue Point, over the tidal race of Sloughnamorro with its standing waves, swirls and strong currents is Fair Head and the serene beauty of Murlough Bay, the last hunting ground for the golden eagle before its demise from these shores.

Road to Rue Point - Rathlin Island

Late Evening Light - Church of St. Thomas

Sunset - Altacarry Lighthouse - Rathlin Island

Fair Head to Rathlin Island

Crannog - Lough na Crannagh

Lough na Crannagh to Knocklayde

Road to Murlough Bay

Fair Head from Torr Head

Torr Head is situated on the scenic coastal road from Ballyvoy, this spectacular headland juts into the North Channel and faces the Mull of Kintyre. On a still day you can hear the roar of the tidal race flowing past the cliffs below, a reminder of the billions of gallons of ocean that ebbs and flows twice a day between Rathlin, Fair Head and the Mull.

The ruin below was once a customs and coastguard station, the lookout on the headland a communications station and coastguard lookout. In 1898 Lloyds of London commissioned Marconi to undertake wireless telegraphy trails between Ballycastle and Rathlin Island, this technology later replaced the old semaphore system at Torr Head to record the arrival and departure of Trans-Atlantic shipping. In summertime flowering currant and fuchsia line the small coastal road as it winds and undulates above the many headlands and bays between Torr and Cushendun.

Ruins of seventeenth century cottages still mark the landscape, bringing a sense of wonder as to how people managed to scratch a living and raise families in such wild and exposed locations, many emigrated during the time of the penal laws and later from the hardships of the famine years. Altagore Cashel on the lower slopes of Cushleake Mountain with its adjacent walled laneway and fields is an intriguing ancient site.

 The coast road then descends into the picturesque village of Cushendun where some fine examples of work by the architect Clough William-Ellis can be found, he also created Portmeirion in Wales, where the 1960s cult television series 'The Prisoner' starring Patrick McGoohan was filmed.

Torr Head and the Mull of Kintyre

Grazing on Green Hill

Portaleen   Harbour

Green Hill to West Torr and Rathlin Island

Runabay Head

Torr Head from Green Hill

Crockan Point, Torr Head and distant Rathlin Island

Cushendun Bay to Red Bay

Altagore Cashel

Architecture by Clough William-Ellis in Cushendun

Cushendun Harbour

Leaving the fertile fields and valleys behind, the inland road gently climbs up through Ballypatrick Forest to Loughareema, known as 'The Vanishing Lake' for its ability to fill and empty within days. Crossing the lake on a causeway, the road then rises to its highest point below Cushleake Mountain where there are excellent views over five of the nine Glens of Antrim.

Glendun is spanned by a viaduct designed by Charles Lanyon and completed in 1839. The stone, quarried near Cushendall was shipped to Cushendun harbour and then taken by horse and cart to the site. It was part of William Bald's 'Grand Military Way' from Larne to Ballycastle. Built in light of strategic lessons learnt by the government after the 1798 uprising, to improve access and allow for the quick deployment of troops, it was later renamed the Antrim Coast Road.

The river Dun and the small road which passes underneath the viaduct follows the whole glen from the tundra like slopes of the plateau, down past evergreen and deciduous woodlands to the sandy beach and harbour of Cushendun. Nearby is Cregagh Wood which contains seventy acres of mixed trees, close to the roadside that skirts the lower part of the wood there is a small worship site known as The Altar in the Woods. A rock with a carved figure of Christ and angel is set into the rock face and is believed to date back to the time of the penal laws. The main road then follows the glen side into Glencorp which joins Glendun and Glenaan.

Townland of Drumadoon

Carey Valley

Loughareema - The Vanishing Lake

Glendun to Glenariffe

The Plateau near Sleiveanorra

Glendun

Abandoned farmstead - Glendun

River Dun

Glendun Viaduct

Altar in the Woods

Cregagh Wood

A little way up Glenaan in the townland of Lubitavish, there is a chamber grave said to be the burial site of Oisin, the poet and warrior son of Finn MacCool. Oisin married and went to live in the mythical land of Tir na nOg, as time passed he became homesick and decided to visit his family, before leaving he was told never to touch the ground or he would die. Arriving in Glenaan, he discovered that 300 years had passed and his family and friends had gone. Returning to Tir na nOg he passed some men trying to move a heavy boulder, he stopped and turned, suddenly the belt holding the saddle broke and he fell to the ground, aged and died. At the entrance to the same field a more recent beehive cairn has been erected to the memory of the Ulster poet John Hewitt known as the poet of the Glens.

Below the slopes of Teiverah with its fairy thorn tree, the Glenaan and Glenballyemon rivers merge to form the Dall which flows through the village of Cushendall. In 1703, the village was part of a forfeited estate bought by the Hollow Sword Blade Company after the Williamite wars. The company, established in 1690 failed but one of its sword smith's went on to form the Mohl Sword Company, later to be taken over by the Wilkinson Sword Company. A Francis Turnley who later owned the village made many improvements, he built several fine buildings including the curfew tower. Built in 1809 as a prison it is said to have been based on chinese towers he had seen while working in Asia for the East India Company.

Abandoned farmstead - Glenaan

Glenaan to the Fairy Hill of Teiverah

The Fairy Thorn - Teiverah

Glenballyemon to Glencorp

Cushendall and Lurigethan Mountain

In a secluded valley overlooking Port Obe and Cushendall Bay is the ruin of the Layde Church. Originally thatched the ruin dates to 1638 and consists of a church and a two story tower which once served as a dormitory. Saint Ciaran was the patron saint and the site is documented as being in use from 1288. A distinct feature of the graveyard is the beautifully carved cross in memory of Doctor James MacDonnell who co-founded the Belfast Medical School.

Near Waterfoot the coast road from Cushendall passes under a red stone arch and on the promontory above with panoramic views in all directions is the ruin of Red Bay Castle. Built on an earlier Norman site, the castle was part of the MacDonnell power base in the mid 1500s and the scene of many battles between the Scotch, Irish and English for control of the Glens until it was finally destroyed by Oliver Cromwell in 1652.

Glenariffe is the largest of the glens and the site of the first narrow gauge railway in Ireland which was built in 1873 by the Glenariffe Iron Ore and Harbour Company. Ore mined in Glenravel was transported down the side of the glen to a purpose built harbour at Carrivemurphy where it was shipped to England and Scotland.

The Glenariffe Forest Park at the head of the glen contains some 1200 hectares of woodland with exceptional walks through varied ecological terrains. The Glenariffe and Inver rivers flow and cascades over waterfalls down the glen until finally merging just past the magnificent and atmospheric 'Tears of the Mountain' waterfall.

Carved Cross to Dr. James MacDonnell

Layde Churchyard - Cushendall

Red Bay Castle

Knockans

Lurigethan Mountain

Early Morning Mist - Glenariffe

Across Glenariffe

Glenariffe River Cascade

Shafts of Light - Glenariffe

Tears of the Mountain - Glenariffe